CARPENTERS for Ukulele

ISBN 978-1-4950-9834-5

HAL•LEONARD®

7777 W. BLUEMOUND RD. P.O. BOX 13819 MILWAUKEE, WI 53213

Visit Hal Leonard Online at
www.halleonard.com

All You Get from Love Is a Love Song

Words and Music by Steve Eaton

§ **Chorus**

dirt - y old shame ___ when all ___ you get from love is a love song ___

___ that's got you lay - in' up nights ___ just wait - in' for the mu - sic to start. ___

___ It's such a dirt - y old shame ___ when you

got to take the blame for a love song, ___ be - cause the

To Coda ⊕

best love songs ___ are writ - ten with a bro - ken heart. ___

1., 2.

3.

D.S. al Coda

⊕ **Coda**

2. And

3. ___

Well, it's a

Bless the Beasts and Children

Words and Music by Barry DeVorzon and Perry Botkin, Jr.

true. So they sprin-kled moon-dust in your hair of gold and star-light in your eyes of

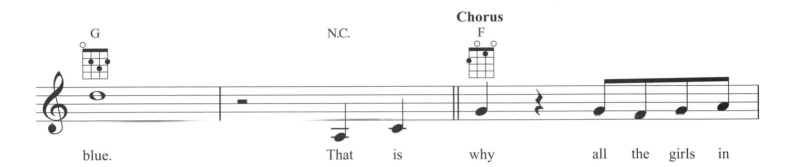

Chorus

blue. That is why all the girls in

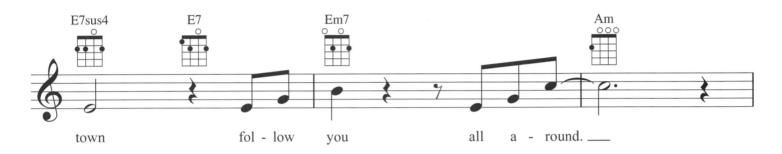

town fol-low you all a-round. ___

To Coda ⊕

Just like me, ___ they long to be close to you. ___

D.S. al Coda
(take 2nd ending)

___ 3. *Instrumental*

⊕ **Coda**

Outro

___ Just like me, ___

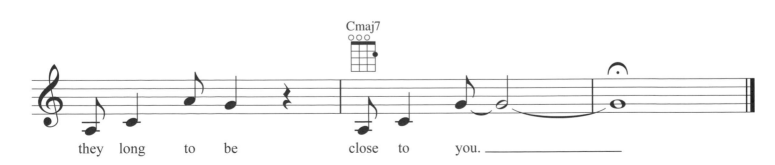

they long to be close to you. ___

For All We Know

from the Motion Picture LOVERS AND OTHER STRANGERS
Words by Robb Wilson and Arthur James
Music by Fred Karlin

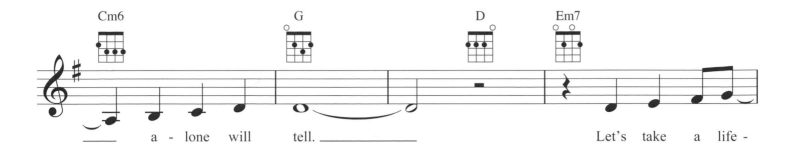

a - lone will tell. _____ Let's take a life -

- time ___ to say,   "I knew you well,"   for on - ly

time _____ will tell us so, _____   and love may

Cmaj7   D7   G   Gmaj7   C

grow,   for   all ___   we   know. _____

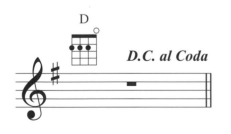

D.C. al Coda

time _____   will   tell   us   so, _____

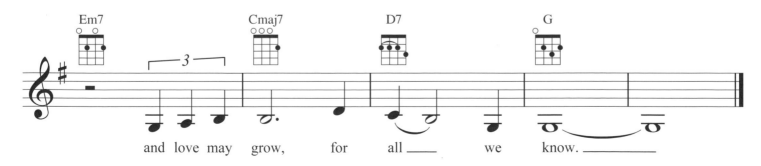

and   love   may   grow,   for   all ___   we   know. _____

Goodbye to Love

Words and Music by Richard Carpenter and John Bettis

Hurting Each Other

Words by Peter Udell
Music by Gary Geld

I Won't Last a Day Without You

Words and Music by Paul Williams and Roger Nichols

world __ has to give, __ but I won't __ last a day __ with - out

1. you. _____ *(Instrumental)*

2. you. Touch me and I end up sing - ing; _____

trou - bles seem to up and dis - ap - pear. You touch me with the love you're

bring - ing. _____ I can't real - ly lose when you're near. (When you're

Verse

near, my __ love.) 3. If all my friends __ have for - got - ten half their prom - is - es, they're

It's Going to Take Some Time

Words and Music by Carole King and Toni Stern

some har - mo - ny. _____ But it's go - ing to take ___ some time ___
                                          It's gon - na take ___ some time ___

_____ this time, ___ and I can't make ___ de - mands. ___
_____ this time, ___ no mat - ter what ___ I've planned. ___
                                                              But like the

young trees in the win - ter - time, ___ I'll learn how ___ to bend. ___

Af - ter all ___ the tears ___ we've spent, ___ how could ___

_____ we make ___ a - mends? So it's one ___ more round ___ for ex - pe -

- ri - ence ___ and I'm on ___ the road ___ a - gain, ___ and it's go -

Only Yesterday

Words and Music by Richard Carpenter and John Bettis

Please Mr. Postman

Words and Music by Robert Bateman, Georgia Dobbins, William Garrett, Freddie Gorman and Brian Holland

so far a-way. ____ Please, Mis-ter Post-man, look and see ____

if there's a let-ter, a let-ter for me. ____ I've been stand-ing here ____

wait-ing, Mis-ter Post-man, so ____ pa-tient - ly, ____

for just a card or just a let-ter, say-ing he's re-turn-ing

Chorus

home ___ to me. ____ Mis - ter Post - man, ____
(Please, Mis - ter Post - man,

____ oh ____ yeah, ____ please, _ please, _
look and see ___ if there's a let-ter in your bag for me. ___

Post - man. Why don't you check it and see ___ one more
Why's it tak - ing such a long time?)

Outro

time for me? ___ You got to wait a min - ute, wait a min - ute.

Wait a min - ute, wait a min - ute. Ooh, _____ Mis - ter Post -
(Mis - ter Post - man,

- man. Come on, de - liv - er the let - ter, the soon - er the bet - ter. _____
look and see.)

_____
(Vocal 1st time only)

Mis - ter Post - man. _____

Repeat and fade

Ah, _____ ah. _____

Rainy Days and Mondays

Lyrics by Paul Williams
Music by Roger Nichols

Merry Christmas, Darling

Words and Music by Richard Carpenter and Frank Pooler

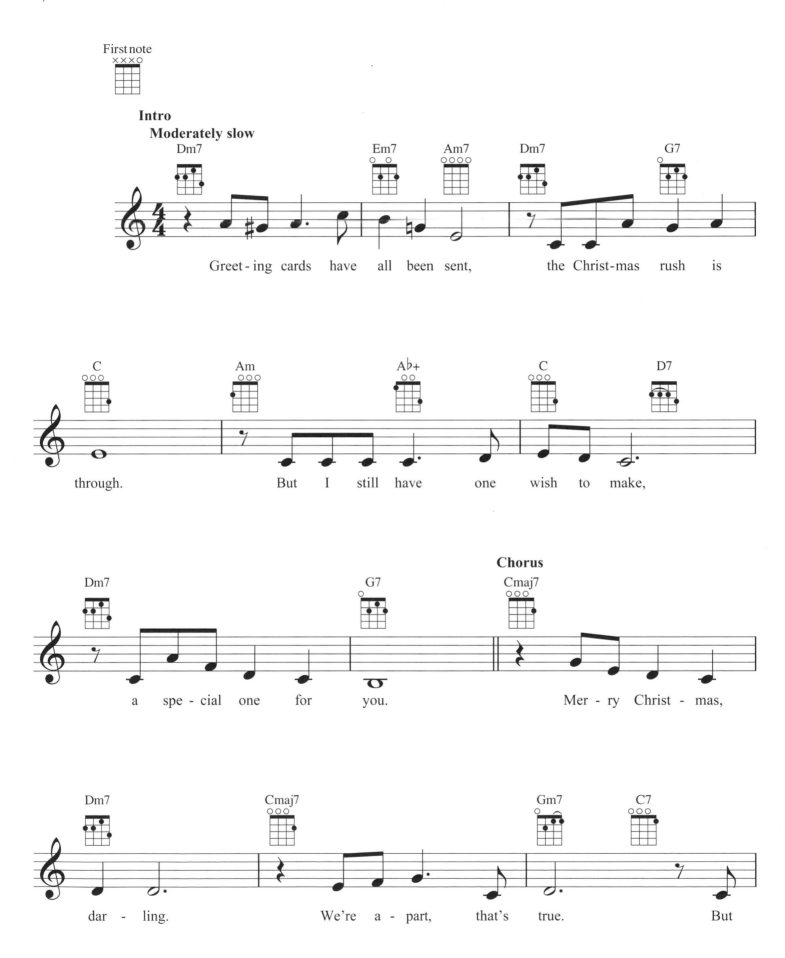

I can dream, and in my dreams, I'm Christ - mas - ing with

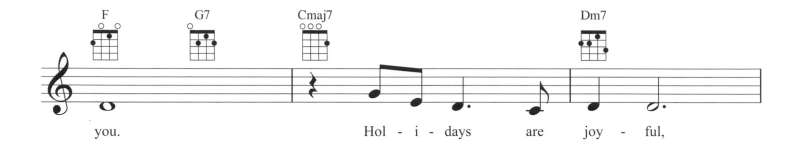

you.   Hol - i - days   are   joy - ful,

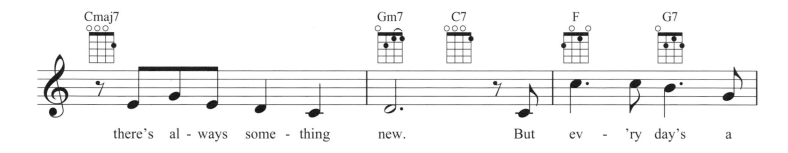

there's al - ways some - thing new.   But   ev - 'ry day's   a

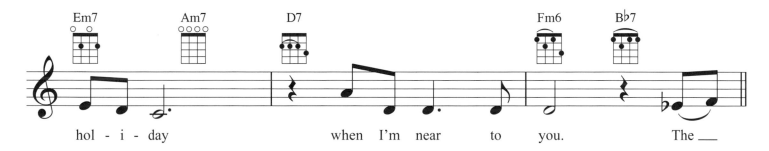

hol - i - day   when I'm near to you.   The ___

Bridge

lights on my tree   I wish you could see,   I wish it ev - 'ry

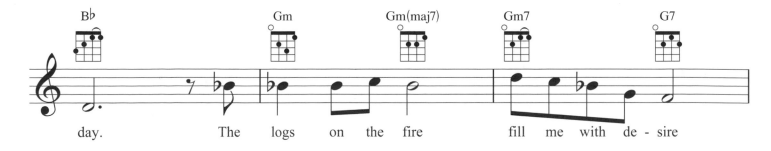

day.   The   logs   on   the   fire   fill   me   with   de - sire

33

Sing

from SESAME STREET
Words and Music by Joe Raposo

Don't wor-ry that it's not good e-nough _ for an-y-one else to

hear; just sing, sing a song. _____

Interlude

Children: La la la la la, la la la la la la, la

Verse

la la la la la la. _____ 2. Sing, sing a

song. Let the world sing a-long. _____

_____ Sing of love there could be.

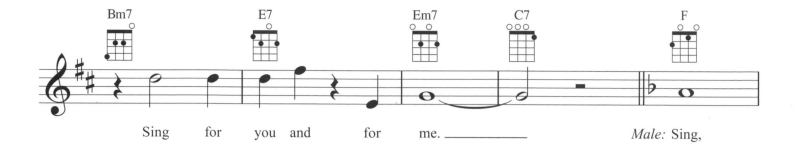

Sing for you and for me. _____ *Male:* Sing,

sing a song. *Female:* Make it sim - ple to last your whole life

long. _____ Don't wor - ry that it's not good e - nough ___ for

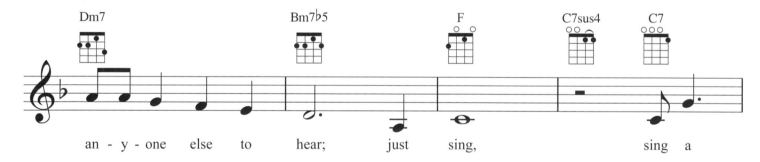

an - y - one else to hear; just sing, sing a

Outro

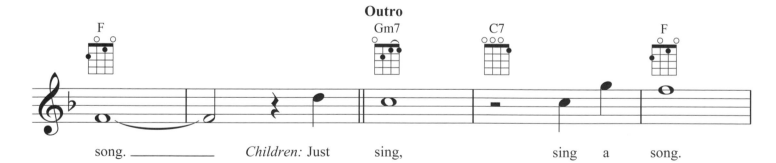

song. _____ *Children:* Just sing, sing a song.

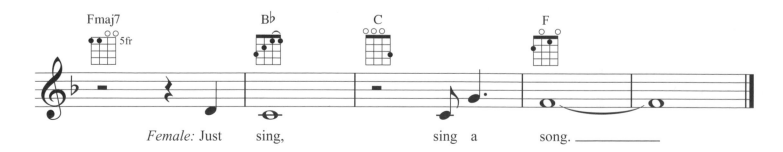

Female: Just sing, sing a song. _____

Solitaire

Words and Music by Neil Sedaka and Phil Cody

died _____ with - in his si - lence. _____
mand _____ the hand he's play - ing.

And

Chorus

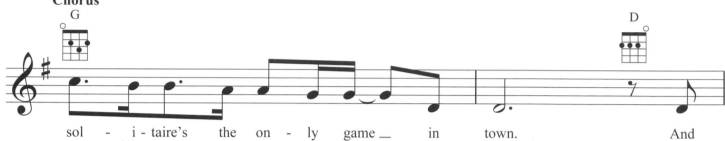

sol - i - taire's the on - ly game ___ in town. And

ev - 'ry road that takes him takes him down. And

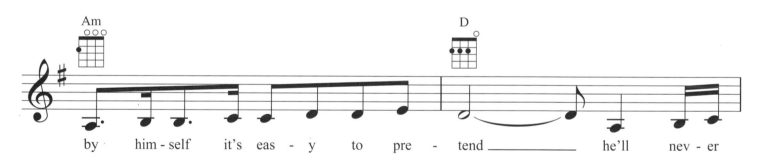

by him - self it's eas - y to pre - tend _____ he'll nev - er

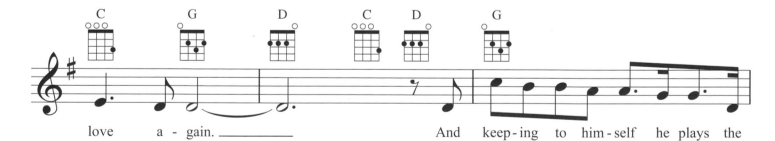

love a - gain. _____ And keep - ing to him - self he plays the

game. With - out _____ her love it al - ways ends the

38

Superstar

Words and Music by Leon Russell and Bonnie Sheridan

There's a Kind of Hush
(All Over the World)

Words and Music by Les Reed and Geoff Stephens

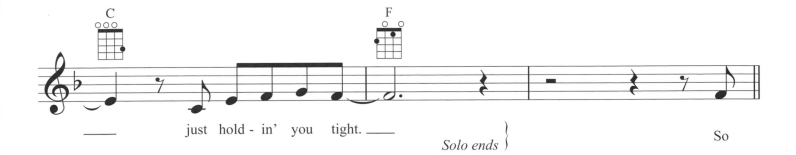

just hold - in' you tight. _____ *Solo ends* So

Bridge

lis - ten ver - y care - ful - ly, _____ get clos - er now _____ and you _____

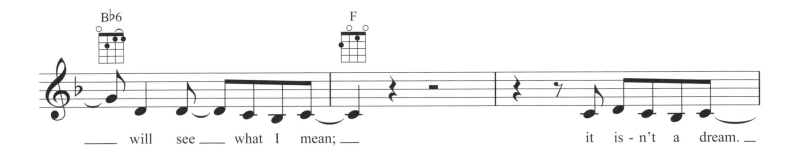

_____ will see _____ what I mean; _____ it is - n't a dream. _____

_____ The on - ly sound that

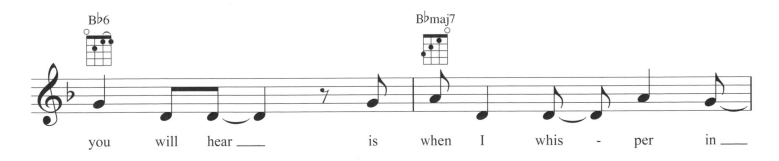

you will hear _____ is when I whis - per in _____

Bb6   C

_____ your   ear, _____ "I   love   you _____

                                              N.C.

for - ev - er   and   ev   -   er." _____   There's a

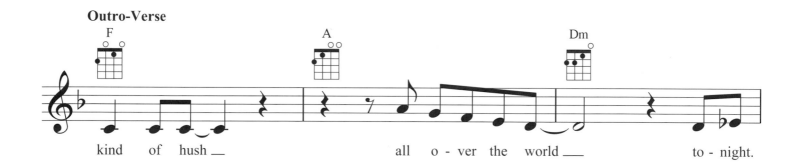

Outro-Verse

F   A   Dm

kind   of   hush ___   all   o - ver   the   world ___   to - night.

F7   Bb

All   o - ver   the   world _____   { peo - ple   just   like   us _____
                                      { you   can   hear   the   sound _

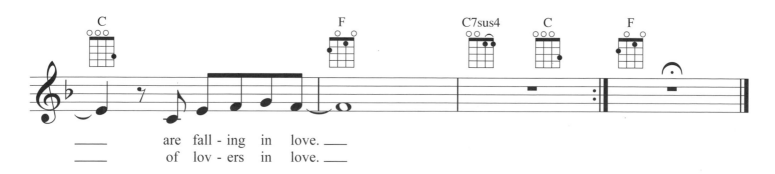

C   F   C7sus4   C   F

_____ are   fall - ing   in   love. ___
_____ of   lov - ers   in   love. ___

Yesterday Once More

Words and Music by John Bettis and Richard Carpenter

back a - gain, ___ just like a long - lost friend, ___ all the
mel - o - dies ___ still sound so good to me ___ as they

songs I love so well. _____
melt the years a - way. _____ } Ev - 'ry

Chorus

sha - la - la - la, ___ ev - 'ry wo ___ wo _____ still shines. _

___ Ev - 'ry shing - a - ling - a - ling that they're

start - in' to sing's _ so fine. _____

{ When they
{ All my

get to the part ___ where he's break - ing her heart, ___ it can
best mem - o - ries ___ come back clear - ly to me, ___ some can

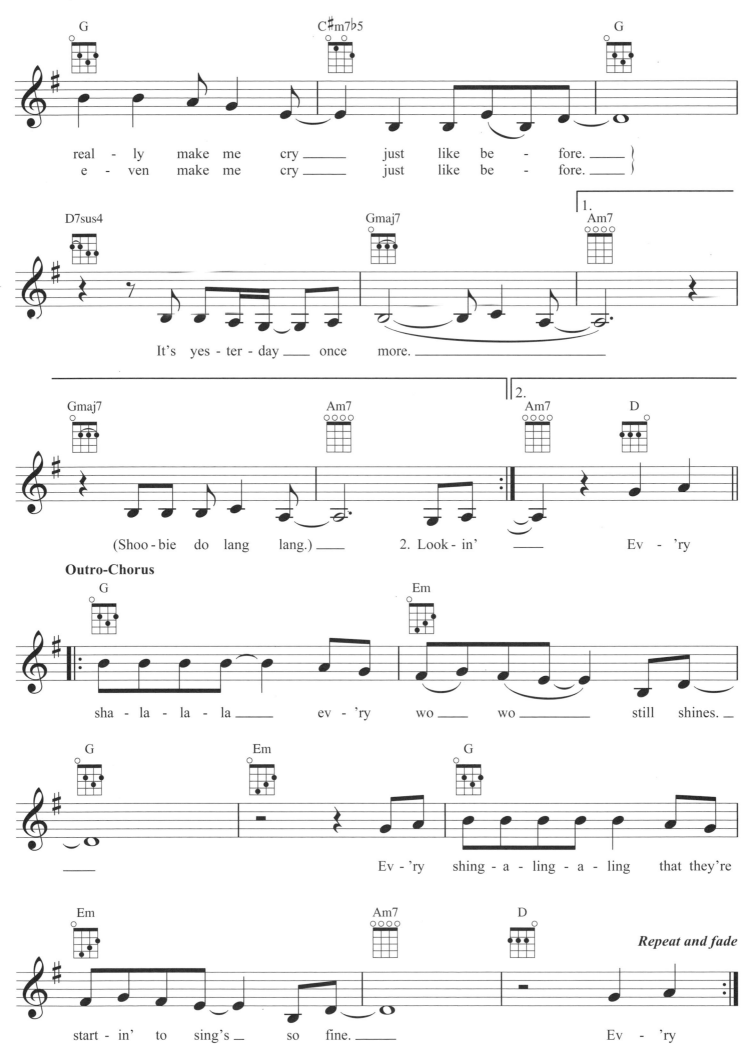

Ticket to Ride

Words and Music by John Lennon and Paul McCartney

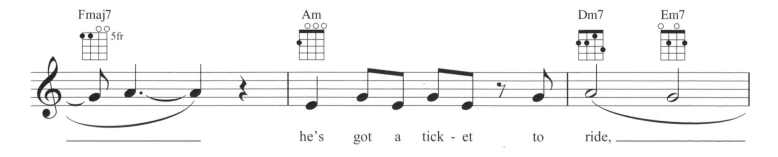

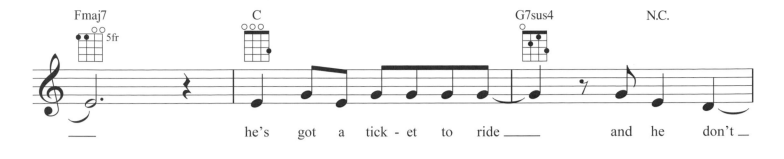

he's got a tick-et to ride _____ and he don't

_____ care. _____

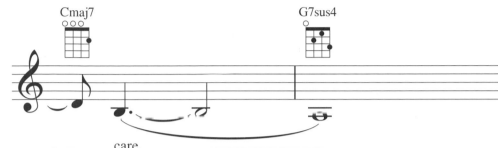

Verse

2. He said that liv-in' with me _____

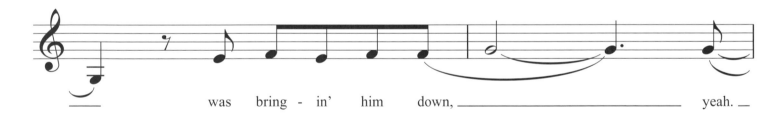

was bring-in' him down, _____ yeah. _____

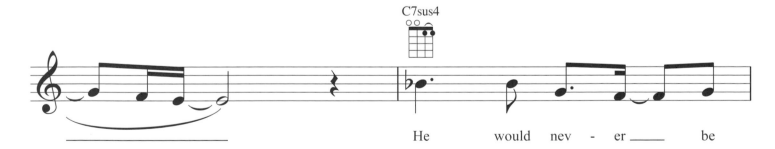

He would nev-er _____ be

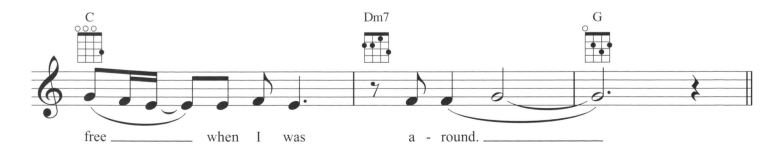

free _____ when I was a - round. _____

We've Only Just Begun

Words and Music by Roger Nichols and Paul Williams

1. We've on-ly just be-gun ___ to live. ___

___ White lace and prom-is-es, a kiss for luck ___ and we're

on our way. ___

2. Be-fore the ris-ing
3., 4. And when the eve-ning

sun, ___ we fly. ___
comes, ___ we smile. ___

So man-y roads to choose;
So much of life a-head;

we start out walk-ing and learn to run. ___
we'll find a place ___ where there's room to grow. ___

And, yes, we've just be - gun. _____

Chorus

Shar - ing ho - ri - zons that are new to us, watch - ing the signs a - long the

way. Talk - ing it o - ver, just the two of us,

work - ing to - geth - er day to day, to - geth - er. _____

D.S. al Coda

geth - er, _____ to - geth - er. _____ And, yes, we've just be -

gun. _____

Top of the World

Words and Music by John Bettis and Richard Carpenter

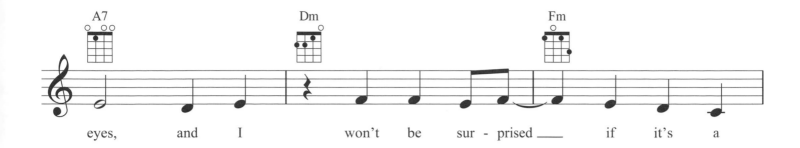

eyes,   and   I   won't   be   sur - prised ____ if   it's   a

1., 3. dream. _____   **2., 4.** seen.   I'm   on   the

Chorus

top   of   the   world _____ look - in'   down   on   cre - a -

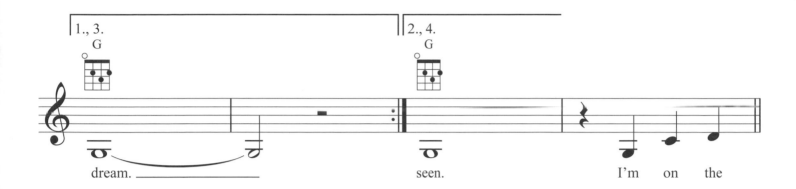

- tion, and the on - ly ex - pla - na - tion I ____ can ____

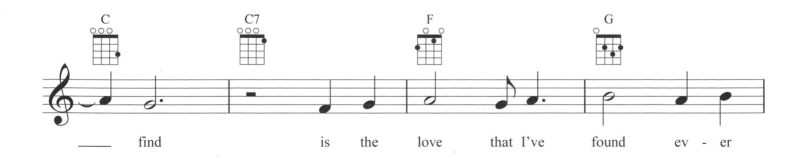

____ find   is   the   love   that I've found   ev - er

since you've been a - round. _____ Your love's put me at the

To Coda ⊕

D.C. al Coda
(with repeat)

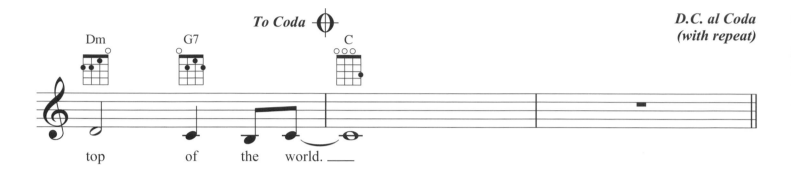

top of the world. _____

⊕ **Coda**

Outro

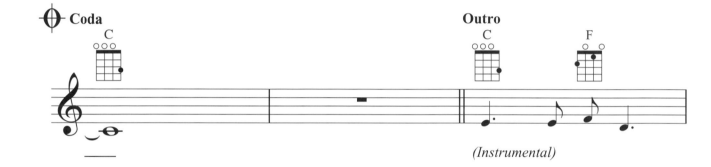

(Instrumental)

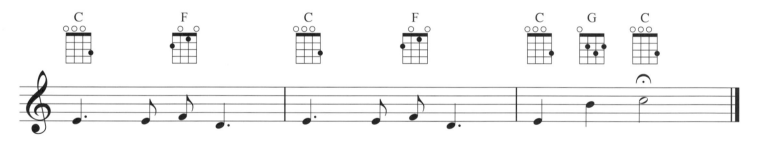

Additional Lyrics

2. Everything I want the world to be
   Is now coming true especially for me.
   And the reason is clear; it's because you are here.
   You're the nearest thing to heaven that I've seen.

3. Something in the wind has learned my name,
   And it's telling me that things are not the same.
   In the leaves on the trees and the touch of the breeze,
   There's a pleasing sense of happiness for me.

4. There is only one wish on my mind:
   When this day is through, I hope that I will find
   That tomorrow will be just the same for you and me.
   All I need will be mine if you are here.